This is the story of the first Pentecost. It is a story of enthusiasm and hope, of courage and renewal in the Apostles and in the people they spoke to.

The Coming of the Holy Spirit

When the day of Pentecost came, all the believers were gathered together in one place. Suddenly there was a noise from the sky which sounded like a strong wind blowing, and it filled the whole house where they were sitting. Then they saw what looked like tongues of fire which spread out and touched each person there. They were all filled with the Holy Spirit and began to talk in other languages, as the Spirit enabled them to speak.

There were Jews living in Jerusalem, religious men who had come from every country in the world. When they heard this noise, a large crowd gathered. They were all excited, because each one of them heard the believers speaking in his own language. In amazement and wonder they exclaimed, 'These people who are talking like this are Galileans! How is it, then, that all of us hear them speaking in our own native languages? We are from Parthia, Media, and Elam; from Mesopotamia, Judaea and Cappadocia; from Pontus and Asia, from Phrygia and Pamphylia, from Egypt and the regions of Libya near Cyrene. Some of us are from Rome, both Jews and Gentiles converted to Judaism, and some of us are from Crete and Arabia – yet all of us hear them speaking in our own languages about the great things that God has done! Amazed and confused they kept asking each other, 'What does this mean?' *(Acts 2:1-12)*

A CONFIRMATION PRAYERBOOK

Come
Holy
Spirit

**Compiled by
Máire Daly**

VERITAS

First published 1993 by
Veritas Publications
7-8 Lower Abbey Street
Dublin 1

Compilation copyright © Máire Daly 1993

Published with ecclesiastical permission
Dublin, 4 January 1993

ISBN 1 85390 265 9

Acknowledgements
The Publishers are grateful to the following for permission to reproduce
their copyright material in this book: McCrimmon Publishing Co. for an
extract from *A Catholic Prayerbook for Schools,* compiled by Michael
Hollings; Lion Publishing for extracts from *The Lion Book of Famous
Prayers,* compiled by Veronica Zundel; The Society for Promoting
Christian Knowledge (SPCK) for extracts from *Tides and Seasons,*
David Adam; The British and Foreign Bible Society for extracts from the
Good News Bible © American Bible Society, New York, 1966, 1971 and
4th edition 1976 published by the Bible Societies/Harper Collins, with
permission; International Committee on English in the Liturgy, Inc.
(ICEL) for excerpts from the English translation of the *Rite of Confirmation*
© 1975, ICEL, excerpts from the English translation of *The Roman Missal*
© 1973, ICEL, an excerpt from the English translation of the *Order of
Christian Funerals* © 1985, ICEL, all rights reserved; Darton, Longman &
Todd Ltd and Doubleday, A division of Bantam Doubleday Dell
Publishing Group Inc. for extracts from *Pocket Book of Prayers,* M. Basil
Pennington © 1986 by Cistercian Abbey of Spencer. Used by permission;
Cistercian Publications, Kalamazoo, Michigan for an excerpt from
Orientations, Thomas Merton, distributed by Mowbray's of Oxford,
England; Christy Kenneally for the poem 'Creation'; Máire Daly for the
prayers on pp. 24, 32, 35, 56, 59, 72,89.

Design by Bill Bolger
Illustrations by Pauline McGrath
Origination by Veritas Publications
Printed in the Republic of Ireland by Betaprint Ltd, Dublin

My dear friends
In Baptism, God our Father gave the new birth of eternal life
to his chosen sons and daughters.
Let us pray to our Father
that he will pour out the Holy Spirit to strengthen his sons and daughters with his gifts and anoint them to be more like Christ, the Son of God.

All-powerful God, Father of our Lord Jesus Christ
by water and the Holy Spirit,
you freed your sons and daughters from sin
and gave them new life.
Send your Holy Spirit upon them
to be their helper and guide.
Give them the spirit of wisdom and understanding,
the spirit of right judgement and courage,
the spirit of knowledge and reverence.
Fill them with the spirit of wonder and awe in your presence.
We ask this through Christ our Lord.
Amen.

I was Confirmed by

Bishop --

Bishop of --

Photograph

Let us pray, that the Gifts of the Holy Spirit, which have been given to us in Confirmation, will become so strong in our lives that wherever we go we will work for God's Kingdom of peace, love, truth and justice.

Holy Spirit, give us the gift of wisdom.
Help us to know always what is the best thing to do.
Help us to know the needs of the people around us.
Help us to find ways of working together as a team for God's Kingdom.

Holy Spirit, give us the gift of understanding.
Help us to understand how people are feeling
deep inside.
Help us never to do anything to hurt others.
Help us especially to understand those whose needs are greater than our own, the very young and the very old, those who are sick and those who are poor.

Holy Spirit, give us the gift of right judgement.
Help us not to be too quick in judging others.
Help us not to be prejudiced.
Help us to be quick to admit when we are wrong.

Holy Spirit, give us the gift of courage.
Help us to continue to do what is right even if others oppose us.
Help us to speak the truth even if it means we must suffer in consequence.
Give us courage especially when life is most difficult, when we are lonely and afraid.

Holy Spirit, give us the gift of knowledge.
Help us to know the reasons why things are as they are.
Help us to know God better.
Help us to know what it is that God wants us to do.

Holy Spirit, give us the gift of reverence.
Help us to love God as Jesus did.
Help us to be aware of God's love for us and enable us to bring this love to others.

Holy Spirit, give us the gift of wonder and awe in God's presence.

Help us to see signs of God's presence in our lives and in the world around us.

Help us to see God in the love and care of our parents and friends.

Help us to see God in new life and growth in the people around us and in the world.

All powerful God, Father of our Lord Jesus Christ, by water and the Holy Spirit you freed your sons and daughters from sin and gave them new life. Send your Holy Spirit upon us to be our helper and guide. Give us the Spirit of wisdom and understanding, the Spirit of right judgement and courage, the Spirit of knowledge and reverence. Fill us with the Spirit of wonder and awe in your presence.

Renewal of Baptismal Promises

Bishop: Do you reject Satan, and all his works, and all his empty promises?

Response: I do.

Bishop: Do you believe in God, the Father almighty, creator of heaven and earth?

Response: I do.

Bishop: Do you believe in Jesus Christ, his only Son, our Lord, who was born of the Virgin Mary, was crucified, died and was buried, rose from the dead, and is now seated at the right hand of the Father?

Response: I do.

Bishop: Do you believe in the Holy Spirit, the Lord, the giver of life, who came upon the apostles at Pentecost and is given to you sacramentally in Confirmation?

Response: I do.

Bishop: Do you believe in the holy catholic church, the communion of saints, the forgiveness of sins, the resurrection of the body, and life everlasting?

Response: I do.

Bishop: This is our faith. This is the faith of the Church. We are proud to profess it in Christ Jesus, our Lord.

Response: Amen.

What Promises would You like to Add?

Think about your life at home, at school and with your friends. Write your promises on this page.

_____

_____

_____

_____

_____

_____

_____

The Fruits of the Holy Spirit

The Gifts of the Holy Spirit bear fruit in our lives.

Love: When we try to live lives full of love for God and for others, when we try to think of and care for other people, we are allowing the Holy Spirit to be active in our lives.

Joy: When we try to be full of joy because of God's goodness to us and when we try to make life happier for others, we are allowing the Holy Spirit to be active in our lives.

Peace: When we try to live in peace with God and with the people around us and when we try to work for peace where there is disagreement, we are allowing the Holy Spirit to be active in our lives.

Patience: When we try to have patience, even in times of hardship, even when things don't go our way, we are allowing the Holy Spirit to be active in our lives. When we wait for others and try to understand that some people may need more time than we do, we are allowing the Holy Spirit to be active in our lives.

Kindness: When we try to be kind to those around us, to care for them, to listen to them, we are allowing the Holy Spirit to be active in our lives.

Goodness: When we try to put the needs of others first and do what is good for them, we are allowing the Holy Spirit to be active in our lives.

Trustfulness: When those around us know that they can trust us and when we trust others and give them a chance, we are allowing the Holy Spirit to be active in our lives.

Gentleness: When we try to be gentle with others, with old people, with our younger brothers and sisters and all those with whom we work and live, we are allowing the Holy Spirit to be active in our lives.

Self-Control: When we try to have self-control so that we don't spoil games or cause trouble at home; when we try to control our temper so that we don't say things in a moment of anger that would hurt others, we are allowing the Holy Spirit to be active in our lives.

Traditional Prayers to the Holy Spirit

Come, Holy Spirit

Come, Holy Spirit, fill the hearts of your faithful, and kindle in them the fire of your love.

Send forth your Spirit and they shall be created, and you will renew the face of the earth.

Let us pray:

O God, on the first Pentecost you filled those who believed in you with the Holy Spirit; under the inspiration of the same Spirit, help us to know what is right and true and give us a sense of your presence and power in our lives always, through Jesus Christ, our Lord.

Amen.

Veni Sancte Spiritus

Come, Holy Spirit,
from heaven shine forth
with your glorious light.
Veni Sancte Spiritus.

✜

Come, Father of the poor,
come, generous Spirit, come,
light of our light.
Veni Sancte Spiritus.

✜

Come from the four winds,
O Spirit, come breath of God;
disperse the shadows over us,
renew and strengthen your people.
Veni Sancte Spiritus.

✜

Father of the poor,
come to our poverty.
Shower upon us the seven gifts of your grace.
Be the light of our lives, o come.
Veni Sancte Spiritus.

✜

Kindle in our hearts the flame of your love,
that in the darkness of the world it may glow
and reach to all forever.
Veni Sancte Spiritus.

O Holy Spirit

O Holy Spirit, give me the stillness of soul in you,
calm the turmoil within me with the gentleness of
your peace.
Quiet the anxiety within me with a deep trust
in you.
Heal the wounds of sin with the joy of your
forgiveness.
Strengthen the faith within, with the awareness of
your presence.
Confirm the hope within, with the knowledge of
your strength.
Give fullness of love within, with outpouring of
your love.
O Holy Spirit, be to me a source of light, strength
and courage so that I may hear your call ever more
clearly and follow it more generously.

Amen.

With my Family on my Confirmation Day

Photograph

Prayers for Every Day

Morning Prayers

Father in heaven, you love me,
you are with me night and day.
I want to love you always
in all I do and say.
I'll try to please you, Father,
Bless me through the day. Amen.

✟

Thank you, Lord, for this day;
For the dawn which is a sign of the sureness of
       your love,
       your presence,
       your forgiveness,
       your companionship,
All the days of our lives.

＋

I start this day in trust in you, Lord.
It may be ordinary,
A day of work or study or even drudgery;
I give it you.

I offer you the hours of this day,
That now or later they may be in your service.

I pray for those I meet.
May I bring in some small way
A dawning of joy and peace in their lives.

Thank you Lord, for this day;
May I always be thankful for what is good.

＋

Good morning, Lord.
Thank you for bringing me to this day.
I put myself into your hands for today.
Direct all my thoughts, words and actions
so that they will be in accordance with your will
and for your honour and glory.

Hail, Mary

Hail, Mary, full of grace,
The Lord is with you.
Blessed are you among women,
And blessed is the fruit of your womb, Jesus.
Holy Mary, mother of God,
Pray for us sinners,
Now and at the hour of our death. Amen.

Sé do bheatha, a Mhuire

Sé do bheatha, a Mhuire,
Atá lán de ghrásta,
Tá an Tiarna leat.
Is beannaithe thú idir mhná,
Agus is beannaithe toradh do bhroinne, Íosa.
A Naomh-Mhuire, a Mháthair Dé,
Guí orainn, na peacaigh,
Anois agus ar uair ár mbáis. Amen.

Glory be to the Father

Glory be to the Father,
And to the Son,
And to the Holy Spirit;
As it was in the beginning,
Is now and ever shall be,
World without end. Amen.

Reflection for the Morning

From behind the clouds the morning sun appears,
and light begins to shine on a new day.
God of the Covenant, I am glad to be able
to start, today, a new task,
to start all over again, in health and good spirits.
I bless you, my God, for the great will to live
and because you accompany me, guide me,
direct my steps, and give me faith.
I am grateful to you for the miracles
we discover at each moment that help us to live
and to use the works of your creation.
Praised be you, my Lord,
for this new day that is born.
Give me your help and guidance.
Guide me with your inspiration, benevolence
and blessing.
Help me to fulfil my duties, and to achieve my aims.
May your light, the divine light, continue to shine
upon me.
May this new day be for me and for everyone
another day of your glory and a day of peace and
happiness. Amen.

The Apostles' Creed

I believe in God,
the Father almighty,
Creator of heaven and earth.

I believe in Jesus Christ, his only Son, our Lord.
He was conceived by the power of the Holy Spirit
And born of the Virgin Mary.
He suffered under Pontius Pilate,
was crucified, died and was buried.
He descended to the dead.
On the third day he rose again.
He ascended into heaven,
And is seated at the right hand of the Father.
He will come again to judge the living and the
dead.

I believe in the Holy Spirit,
The holy catholic Church,
The communion of saints,
The forgiveness of sins,
The resurrection of the body,
And life everlasting.
Amen.

Grace before Meals

Bless us, O God, as we sit together.
Bless the food we eat today.
Bless the hands that made the food.
Bless us, O God. Amen.

☩

Father, bless us and bless our food; bless all those
who make it possible for us to enjoy your gifts. And,
Father, we pray, too, for our hungry sisters and
brothers everywhere. Teach us to share so that no
one will hunger on this your bountiful earth. Amen.

Grace after Meals

Thank you, God, for the food we have eaten.
Thank you, God, for all our friends.
Thank you, God, for everything.
Thank you, God, Amen.

☩

We thank you, God, for all your gifts and praise
you, as all who live must praise you each day; for
you teach us in your Scriptures: 'When you have
eaten your fill, you shall praise God for the good
land that God has given you.' Holy One of
Blessing, we thank you for the land and its fruit.

Our Father

Our Father, who art in heaven,
Hallowed be thy name.
Thy Kingdom come.
Thy will be done on earth, as it is in heaven.
Give us this day our daily bread,
And forgive us our trespasses,
As we forgive those who trespass against us,
And lead us not into temptation,
But deliver us from evil.
Amen.

Ár nAthair

Ár nAthair, atá ar neamh,
Go naofar d'ainm,
Go dtaga do Ríocht,
Go ndéantar do thoil ar an talamh
Mar a dhéantar ar neamh.
Ár n-arán laethúil tabhair dúinn inniu;
Agus maith dúinn ár bhfiacha,
Mar a mhaithimidne dár bhféichiúna féin,
Agus ná lig sinn i gcathú,
Ach saor sinn ó olc.
Amen.

Evening Prayers

God our Father, I come to say,
Thank you for your love today.
Thank you for my family,
And all the friends you give to me.
Guard me in the dark of night,
And in the morning send your light. Amen.

✝

Forgive me, O God,
    For the time I have wasted today;
    For the people I have hurt today;
    For the tasks I have shirked today.
Help me
    Not to be discouraged when things are difficult
    Not to be content with second best;
    To do better tomorrow than I have done today.
And help me always to remember that Jesus is
with me and that I am not trying all alone.
This I ask for Jesus' sake. Amen.

This evening, Lord, I give you thanks.
For the good things of today,
for people whose friendship I value,
for the work well done,
for deadlines met,
for home and for shelter,
for the food I ate.
Thank you, Lord.

For today, Lord, thanks and sorry.
I put to rest with you the troubles of this day;
I ask the peace of your presence until the new day
dawns.
May the protection you give at the end of a day
Be with me and my loved ones
All the days of our lives.

Reflection for the Evening

At the beginning of another night,
thank you, Lord, for all the good things of today.
For the sun which brings light and life
to the world.
For the beautiful world I live in with all its shapes
and colours and many life forms.
For all the people who love and care for me,
my family, my friends, and all those who
contribute to my happiness in any way.
For the food and water which keep my body
strong and healthy.
Knowing that you are present with me, may I also
help others to become more aware of your
constant love and presence in their lives.

With My Friends

Photograph

When I Need Courage

Lord, help me always to remember the words
you said,
'I will be with you always.'
Knowing this and confident of your guiding
presence, help me to be
truthful and honest even when others are not.
Help me to forgive those who injure or hurt me.
Give me the strength and confidence
to reach out to others in need, particularly
when it is most difficult.
Above all, give me the courage always to
do what is right, even when others
pressurise or ridicule me.

Grant Me, O Lord

Grant me, O Lord,
The courage to change the things that I can,
The serenity to accept the things that I cannot,
And the wisdom to know the difference.

'My commandment is this: Love one another, just as I love you.' (John 15:12)

Love is patient and kind;
it is not jealous or conceited or proud;
Love is not ill-mannered or selfish or irritable;
Love does not keep a record of wrongs;
Love is not happy with evil,
but is happy with the truth.
Love never gives up;
and its faith, hope and patience never fail.
Love is eternal. (*1 Corinthians 13:4-8*)

St Patrick's Breastplate

Christ be with me,
Christ be beside me,
Christ be before me,
Christ be behind me,
Christ be at my right hand,
Christ be at my left hand,
Christ be with me everywhere I go.
Christ be my friend, for ever and ever.
Amen.

Prayer of Thanks for Friends

Thank you, Lord, for the gift of friendship.
For the times I spend with my friends;
For the times when we have fun together;
For the times when we work together.
Thank you for the companionship I experience
from my friends.
My friends are people who know me and care for
me as I am.
Thank you for their friendship especially at times
when I feel lonely or sad or afraid.
Help me to be a good friend in return.
Help me to follow the example of Jesus,
when he was prepared to give even his life for his
friends, so that I will be prepared to put the needs
of my friends before my own.

What the Bible says about Friendship

Love one another, just as I love you. The greatest love a person can have for his friends is to give his life for them. (*John 15:12-13*)

A loyal friend is like a safe shelter;
find one and you have found a treasure.
(*Sirach 6:14*)

Friends always show their love. (*Proverbs 17*)

A friend means well, even when he hurts you.
(*Proverbs 27:6*)

If you are polite and courteous, you will enjoy the friendship of many people. (*Sirach 6:5*)

A person who listens to the Lord will find real friends, because he will treat his friends as he does himself. (*Sirach 6:17*)

I will never be afraid to protect a friend and I will never turn a friend away if he needs me.
(*Sirach 22:25*)

Write your own Friendship Motto:

_____

_____

_____

_____

_____

Photograph of my Friends

Photograph

Gloria

Glory to God in the highest,
And peace to his people on earth.

Lord God, heavenly King,
Almighty God and Father,
We worship you, we give you thanks,
We praise you for your glory.

Lord Jesus Christ, only Son of the Father,
Lord God, Lamb of God,
You take away the sin of the world:
Have mercy on us;
You are seated at the right hand of the Father:
Receive our prayer.

For you alone are the Holy One,
You alone are the Lord,
You alone are the Most High, Jesus Christ,
With the Holy Spirit
in the glory of God, the Father.
Amen.

Prayers in Praise of Creation

God looked at everything he had made, and he was very pleased. (Genesis 1:31)

Thanks for Creation

O God, we thank you for this earth, our home;
for the wide sky and the blessed sun, for the salt sea
and the running water, for the everlasting hills and
the never-resting winds, for trees and the common
grass underfoot.

We thank you for our senses
by which we hear the songs of birds, and see the
splendour of the summer fields, and taste of the
autumn fruits, and rejoice in the feel of the snow
and smell the breath of the spring.

Grant us a heart wide open to all this beauty;
and save our souls from being so blind that we pass
unseeing when even the common thornbush is
aflame with your glory,
O God, our Creator, who lives and reigns for ever
and ever.

The Canticle of Brother Sun

Be praised, my Lord, for all your creatures.
In the first place for the blessed Brother Sun,
who gives us the day and enlightens us
through you.
He is beautiful and radiant with his great
splendour.
Giving witness to you, most Omnipotent One.

Be praised, my Lord, for Sister Moon and the stars
formed by you so bright, precious and beautiful.

Be praised, my Lord, for Brother Wind and the
airy skies, so cloudy and serene; for every weather
be praised, for it is life-giving.

Be praised, my Lord, for Sister Water, so necessary,
yet so precious, humble and chaste.

Be praised, my Lord, for Brother Fire, who lights
up the night. He is beautiful and carefree, robust
and fierce.

Be praised, my Lord, for our sister, Mother Earth,
who nourishes and watches us while bringing
forth abundance of fruits with coloured flowers
and herbs.

Be praised, my Lord, for those who pardon
through your love and bear weaknesses and trial.
Blessed are those who endure in peace, for they will
be crowned by you, Most High.

Be praised, my Lord, for our sister, Bodily Death,
whom no living man can escape. Woe to those who
die in sin.
Blessed are those who discover your holy will.
The second death will do them no harm.

Praise and bless the Lord.
Render thanks.
Serve him with great humility.
Amen.

Creation

Long ago, long, long ago,
When all was darkness deep and low,
The voice of God called forth the light
To split the curtain of the night.
Then what was light he called the day
While what was night in darkness lay.

Then God divided earth and sea
And marked the place where each should be
With mountains rising high and steep
And oceans spreading wide and deep.

Then God called seeds to sprout and grow
And all the flowers that we know.
The trees and grass both great and small
Blossomed when they heard his call.

Then God said 'Let the darkest night
Be filled with tiny glowing lights'.
He called the sun to light the day,
The moon to keep the dark away.

Then God called all that swim and fly,
The creatures of the sea and sky,
And all the creatures of the land
Were shaped and formed by God's good hands.

When all was done God loved it all,
The dew drop and the waterfall,
The timid creatures and the strong,
The robin and the thrush's song.

He searched the sea and sky above
To find one who would share his love.
When none was found his plan unfurled,
God made a man to share his world.
He made a man and woman too
To share his world so bright and new;

To love the earth, the sea and sky,
The creatures, fish and birds that fly.
God gave them all to man to show
His special love, long, long ago.

God's Glory

O Lord, our Lord,
your greatness is seen in all the world!
Your praise reaches up to the heavens.

When I look at the sky, which you have made;
at the moon and the stars, which you set in their
place – what are we, that you think of us, that you
care for us?

Yet you made us inferior only to yourself;
you crowned us with glory and honour.
You appointed us ruler over everything you made;
you placed us over all creation: sheep, cattle,
and the wild animals too;
the birds and the fish and the creatures in the seas.

O Lord, our Lord,
your greatness is seen in all the world!

Traditional Irish Prayers in Praise of Creation

Maker of All

You are the Maker
Of earth and sky,
You are the Maker
Of heaven on high.
You are the Maker
Of oceans deep,
You are the Maker
Of mountains steep.
You are the Maker
Of sun and rain,
You are the Maker
Of hill and plain.
You are the Maker
Of such as me.
Keep me, O Lord
Eternally.
Teach me to see you, Lord,
In all things seen and heard,
In beauty of the heather moors,
In the singing of a bird.

Creator God

What makes the sun to rise?
The power of God.

What makes the seed to grow?
The love of God.

What makes the wind to blow?
The Spirit of God.

Power of God protect us.
Love of God lead us.
Spirit of God strengthen us,
In all of life
And all creation.

My own Prayer in Praise of Creation

_____

_____

_____

_____

_____

_____

_____

_____

Prayers for Vocations

A prayer of Thomas Merton

My Lord God, I have no idea where I am going.

I do not see the road ahead of me. I cannot know
for certain where it will end.

Nor do I really know myself, and the fact that I
think that I am following your will does not
mean that I am actually doing so.

But I believe that the desire to please you does in
fact please you.

And I hope that I have that desire in all that
I am doing.

I hope that I will never do anything apart from
that desire.

And I know that if I do this you will lead me by the
right road though I may know nothing about it.

Therefore I will trust you always though I may
seem to be lost in the shadow of death.

I will not fear, for you are ever with me, and will
never leave me to face my perils alone.

To do what is good with my life

Lord, I really want to do something good with
my life.
I see the needs of the world I'm part of,
  one million poor in my own country,
  people killed each day through violence,
  old people living lonely and in squalour,
  kids of my own age drugging themselves
  as an escape from life.

I hear your call,
Sometimes a whisper, other times a gentle shove
Inviting me to be your presence,
Through my own personality and my own talents
And with all my weaknesses,
In the world of these people.
But, Lord, I'm afraid.
  I don't know if I can do anything for them.
  I don't know how you want me to follow you:
  Married? single? a religious? a priest?
I'm not sure I can give without losing so much myself.
Faith is what I ask, and light and love:
Faith to believe in your risen power at the foot of
your cross,
Light to know the way you're asking me to serve you,
And love to trust that it's all possible.

Prayers Before Communion

Lord Jesus, come to me.
Lord Jesus, give me your love.
Lord Jesus, come to me and give me yourself.

Act of Faith

Lord Jesus Christ, I firmly believe that you are present in this blessed sacrament, as true God and true man, with your body and blood, your soul and divinity. My redeemer and my judge, I adore your divine majesty together with the angels and saints. I believe, O Lord; increase my faith.

Act of Hope

Good Jesus, in you alone I place all my hope. You are my salvation and my strength, the source of all good. Through your mercy, through your Passion and Death, I hope to obtain the pardon of my sins, the grace of final perseverance, and a happy eternity.

Act of Love

Jesus, my God, I love you with my whole heart
and above all things, because you are the one
supreme Good and an infinitely perfect God.
You have given your life for me, a poor sinner, and
in your mercy you have even offered yourself as
food for my soul.
My God, I love you.
Inflame my heart so that I may love you more.

Prayers After Communion

For Love towards Others

Keep me from smallness of mind, O Lord,
Let me be big in thought, in word and in action.
Let me be finished for ever with fault-finding
and self-love.
May I put away all pretending and meet everyone
face to face without self-pity or deceit.
May I never be hasty in judging and may I be
always generous.
Let me take time for all things.
Make me grow calm, peaceful and gentle.
Teach me to put into action my good desires.
Teach me to be straightforward and fearless.
Grant that I may realise that it is the little things of
life that make difficulties and divisions and that in
the big things of life we are one.
And, O Lord God, do not let me forget to be kind.
My God, make us all of one mind in the truth and
of one heart in love. Amen.

Prayer for Holiness

Give me, O God,
understanding to know you,
perseverance to seek you,
and wisdom to find you.
Give me a life that will please you,
and a hope that will unite me to you when I die.
Amen.

Jesus, I believe that I have received your flesh to eat
and your blood to drink,
because you have said it and your word is true.

Lord Jesus, I love and adore you,
You're a special friend to me.
Welcome, Lord Jesus, O welcome!
Thank you for coming to me.

The Confiteor

I confess to almighty God,
And to you, my brothers and sisters,
That I have sinned through my own fault,
in my thoughts and in my words,
in what I have done,
And in what I have failed to do;
And I ask blessed Mary, ever virgin,
All the angels and saints,
And you my brothers and sisters,
To pray for me to the Lord our God. Amen.

Prayers of Sorrow

Act of Sorrow

O my God, I thank you for loving me.
I am sorry for all my sins:
For not loving others and not loving you.
Help me to live like Jesus and not sin again. Amen.

My God,
I am sorry for my sins with all my heart.
In choosing to do wrong and failing to do good,
I have sinned against you
whom I should love above all things.
I firmly intend, with your help,
to do penance, to sin no more,
and to avoid whatever leads me to sin.
Our Saviour, Jesus Christ, suffered and died for us.
In his name, my God, have mercy.
Father, I have sinned against you
and am not worthy to be called your child.
Be merciful to me, a sinner.

✛

Lord God, our loving Father,
you know all my weaknesses and failures.
I come to you with deep sorrow in my heart.
Forgive me,
accept me,
strengthen me.

✛

Forgive me, Lord, for all the wrong I have done
this day.
Forgive me for being bad-tempered and hard to
live with.
Forgive me for hurting those I should love.
Forgive me for making life difficult for others.
Forgive me for the words of comfort and praise and
thanks which I should have spoken but did not
speak.
Forgive me for the help I should have given to
those in need and did not give.
God of mercy, be merciful to me a sinner.
Amen.

Examination of Conscience

Have I neglected to spend time
thanking God for his goodness to me?
Have I spoken disrespectfully of God or of Jesus?
Have I forgotten or been too busy to say my
prayers?
Have I been careless at Mass,
by not listening or by distracting others?
Have I thought only of my own needs and not
considered the needs of others:
by going out to play instead of helping at home;
by keeping things for myself instead of sharing
with others;
by taking more than my fair share of something
that should have been divided among others?
Have I been jealous of the things that others own
or of the gifts or talents of another?
Have I misused or refused to use the gifts and
talents that I have been given?
Have I done something in anger?
Have I been unjust?
Have I taken things that didn't belong to me?
Have I left others out of games when I knew they
were lonely and needed friendship?

Have I looked down on others?
Have I told lies?
Have I spread rumours about another person?
Have I shown disrespect for those who have
authority over me by disobeying my parents or my
teachers?
Have I shown disrespect for my own body or
another person's body?
Have I used disrespectful language when talking to
or about another person?
Have I tried to get my own back on another?

My God,
I firmly intend, with your help, to change my
heart, to sin no more and to avoid whatever leads
me to sin.

Come, Holy Spirit,
lead me, in faith, to the healing
and pardon that Christ, my Saviour, has for me in
this Sacrament of Penance; bring me to the
welcome of the Father whom I have offended.

A Prayer to Thank God for Happy Times

Thank you, Lord for all the things that bring me
happiness;
for friendship
for fun and games
for birthday parties and celebrations
for books to read
for the countryside and all its beauty
for the seaside in summer time.

May I always be aware of the many blessings which
you have given me.
Help me always to add something to the world's
beauty and to the world's joy.
Through Jesus Christ, my Lord. Amen.

A Happy Time with my Family and with my Friends

Photograph

Prayers in Honour of Mary

Hail, Holy Queen

Hail, holy Queen, mother of mercy;
Hail our life, our sweetness, and our hope!
To you we cry, poor banished children of Eve;
To you we send up our sighs,
mourning and weeping in this valley of tears.
Turn then, most gracious advocate,
Your eyes of mercy towards us;
And after this our exile,
Show to us the blessed fruit of your womb, Jesus.
O clement, O loving, O sweet Virgin Mary.
Pray for us, O holy Mother of God,
that we may be made worthy of the promises of
Christ.

The Angelus

The Angel of the Lord declared unto Mary
And she conceived of the Holy Spirit.
Hail Mary...

Behold the handmaid of the Lord.
Be it done unto me according to thy word.
Hail Mary...

And the word was made flesh
And dwelt among us.
Hail Mary...

Pray for us, O Holy Mother of God,
That we may be made worthy of the promises of
Christ.

Lord, fill our hearts with your love,
And as you revealed to us by an angel
The coming of your Son as man,
So lead us through his suffering and death
To the glory of his resurrection,
For he lives and reigns with you and the Holy Spirit,
One God, for ever and ever. Amen.

The Memorare

Remember, O most gracious Virgin Mary,
that never was it known
that anyone who fled to your protection,
implored your help, or sought your intercession
was left unaided.
Inspired with this confidence,
I fly unto you, O Virgin of virgins, my Mother.
To you I come, before you I stand, sinful and
sorrowful.
O Mother of the Word incarnate,
despise not my petitions,
but in your mercy, hear and answer me.
Amen.

The Mysteries of the Rosary

The Joyful Mysteries

The Annunciation
The Visitation
The Birth of our Lord
The Presentation of our Lord in the Temple
The Finding of our Lord in the Temple

The Sorrowful Mysteries

The Agony of our Lord in the Garden
The Scourging at the Pillar
The Crowning with Thorns
The Carrying of the Cross
The Crucifixion and the Death of our Lord

The Glorious Mysteries

The Resurrection of our Lord
The Ascension of our Lord into Heaven
The Descent of the Holy Spirit upon the Apostles
The Assumption of Our Lady into Heaven
The Crowning of Our Lady as Queen of Heaven.

The Magnificat

My soul glorifies the Lord,
My spirit rejoices in God, my Saviour.
He looks on his servant in her lowliness;
Henceforth all ages will call me blessed.

The Almighty works marvels for me.
Holy his name!
His mercy is from age to age,
On those who fear him.

He puts forth his arm in strength
And scatters the proud-hearted.
He casts the mighty from their thrones
And raises the lowly.

He fills the starving with good things,
Sends the rich away empty.

He protects Israel, his servant,
Remembering his mercy,
The mercy promised to our fathers,
To Abraham and his sons for ever. Amen.

Prayers from Irish Spirituality

With you, Lord

You are to be found in our lives,
Help us to seek you.

You do wonders among us,
Help us to see you.

You reign over the world,
Help us to obey you.

You triumph over all,
Help us to rise with you.

You enter your Kingdom,
Help us to live with you.

Be Opened

Lord, open our lips,
And our mouth shall declare your praise.

Lord, open our eyes,
And our seeing shall behold your glory.

Lord, open our hearts,
And our feeling shall know your love.

Lord, open our minds,
And our thinking shall discover your wonders.

Lord, open our hands,
And our giving shall show your generosity.

Lord, open our lives,
And our living shall declare your Presence.

Prayers for Peace

Lord Jesus Christ,
You said to your apostles:
I leave you peace,
my peace I give you.
Look not on our sins,
but on the faith of your Church,
and grant us the peace and unity of your Kingdom
Where you live for ever and ever.
Amen.

Prayer of St Francis of Assisi

Lord, make me an instrument of your peace.
Where there is hatred let me sow love;
Where there is injury, pardon;
Where there is doubt, faith;
Where there is despair, hope;
Where there is darkness, light;
And where there is sadness, joy.

O Divine Master,
grant that I may not so much seek
To be consoled as to console;
To be understood as to understand;
To be loved as to love;
For it is in giving that we receive;
It is in pardoning that we are pardoned;
And it is in dying that we are born
to eternal life.

The Benedictus

Blessed be the Lord, the God of Israel!
He has visited his people and redeemed them.

He has raised up for us a mighty Saviour
in the house of David his servant,
as he promised by the lips of holy men,
those who were his prophets from of old.

A Saviour who would free us from our foes,
from the hands of all who hate us.
So his love for our fathers is fulfilled
and his holy covenant remembered.

He swore to Abraham, our father to grant us,
that free from fear,
and saved from the hands of our foes,
we might serve him in holiness and justice
all the days of our life in his presence.

As for you, little child,
you shall be called a prophet of God,
the Most High.

You shall go ahead of the Lord
to prepare his ways before him,
To make known to his people
their salvation through forgiveness of all their sins,
the loving kindness of the heart of our God
who visits us like the dawn from on high.

He will give light to those in darkness,
those who dwell in the shadow of death,
and guide us into the way of peace.

Come, my young friends, and listen to me,
and I will teach you to honour the Lord.
Would you like to enjoy life?
Do you want long life and happiness?
Then hold back from speaking evil
and from telling lies.
Turn away from evil and do good;
strive for peace with all your heart.

Dear Lord,

We pray for those whose families, homes and lives have been devastated by the violence and hatred in our country.
Give healing and hope to all who are in distress.

We pray for those caught up in the spiral of intolerance, bigotry and murder.
Touch their hearts with the reconciling power of your love.

Give to our troubled world your gift of peace.
Bring all people together in unity and love.
Let us experience your healing presence and lead us back to you and make us holy.

We pray that we may be filled with faith and courage, simplicity and peace;
In your mercy, hear our prayer.

My Own Prayer for Peace

_____

_____

_____

_____

_____

_____

_____

_____

_____

The Beatitudes

Blessed are the poor in spirit:
theirs is the Kingdom of Heaven.

Blessed are the gentle:
they shall have the earth for their heritage.

Blessed are those who mourn:
they shall be comforted.

Blessed are those who hunger and thirst
for what is right:
they shall be satisfied.

Blessed are the merciful:
they shall have mercy shown them.

Blessed are the pure in heart:
they shall see God.

Blessed are the peacemakers:
they shall be called children of God.

Blessed are those who are persecuted
in the cause of right: theirs is the Kingdom of Heaven.

Blessings

May the Lord bless you and keep you.

May his face shine upon you, and be gracious to you.

May the God of all consolation bless you in every way and grant you peace all the days of your life.

May he free you from all anxiety and strengthen your hearts in his love.

May he enrich you with his gifts of faith, hope and love, so that what you do in this life will bring you to the happiness of everlasting life.

May almighty God bless you, the Father and the Son and the Holy Spirit.

Amen.

Traditional Irish Blessings

May the road rise to meet you,
may the wind be always at your back,
may the sun shine warm on your face,
the rain fall softly on your fields;
and until we meet again,
may God hold you in the palm of his hand.

And With Your Spirit

The Lord be with you. *And with your spirit too.*

Today, tonight
In shade and light
The Lord be with you. *And with your spirit too.*

In weakness and pain,
In powers that wane,
The Lord be with you. *And with your spirit too.*

In health and in might,
In strength for the fight,
The Lord be with you. *And with your spirit too.*

In your coming to rest,
In rising with the blessed,
The Lord be with you. *And with your spirit too.*

Christ's Body

Christ has no body now on earth but yours;

Yours are the only hands with which he can do his work,

Yours are the only feet with which he can go about the world,

Yours are the only eyes through which his compassion can shine forth upon a troubled world.

Christ has no body now on earth but yours.

Teresa of Avila

The Lord Is My Shepherd

The Lord is my shepherd;
I have everything I need.
He lets me rest in fields of green grass
and leads me to quiet pools of fresh water.
He gives me new strength.
He guides me in the right paths,
as he has promised.
Even if I go through the deepest darkness,
I will not be afraid, Lord,
for you are with me.
Your shepherd's rod and staff protect me.

You prepare a banquet for me,
where all my enemies can see me;
you welcome me as an honoured guest
and fill my cup to the brim.
I know that your goodness and love
will be with me all my life;
and your house will be my home
as long as I live.
(Psalm 23)

———

A Prayer of Thanksgiving

I thank you, Lord, with all my heart,
you have heard the words of my mouth.
Before the angels I will bless you,
I will adore before your holy temple.

I thank you for all your faithfulness and love,
which excel all we ever knew of you.
On the day I called, you answered;
you increased the strength of my soul.

All earth's kings shall thank you
when they hear the words of your mouth.
They shall sing of the Lord's ways:
'How great is the glory of the Lord!'

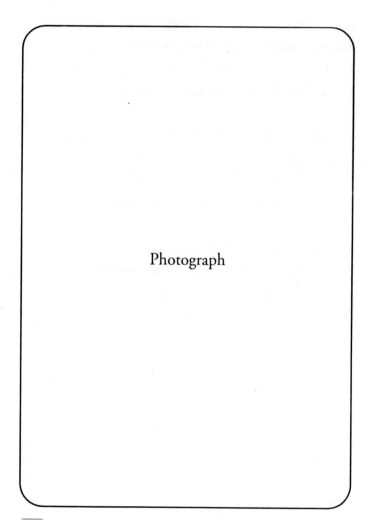

Photograph

The Stations of the Cross

Jesus loved his Father and trusted him always. He devoted himself to bringing people back to his Father's love. This was his mission in life. Nothing could stop him from loving his Father and trusting him, neither difficulties, nor hatred, nor even death. Jesus said: 'A man can have no greater love than to give his life for his friends.'

God the Father raised Jesus to a new and glorious life. Jesus is alive. He is risen from the dead. He is now happy with his Father.

1 Jesus is condemned to death
2 Jesus takes up his cross
3 Jesus falls the first time

We worship you, Lord.
We venerate your cross.
We praise your resurrection.
Through your cross you brought joy to the world.
May God be gracious and bless us
And may his love shed its light upon us.

Jesus remember me,
When you come into your kingdom.
Jesus remember me,
When you come into your kingdom.

We adore you, O Christ, and we bless you;
because by your holy cross
you have redeemed the world.

10 Jesus is stripped of his garments
11 Jesus is nailed to the cross
12 Jesus dies on the cross

It was now about the sixth hour, and there was darkness over the whole land until the ninth hour while the sun's light failed; and the curtain of the temple was torn in two. Then Jesus, crying out with a loud voice said, 'Father into thy hands I commend my spirit!' and having said this he breathed his last. *(Luke 23:44-46)*

13 Jesus is taken down from the cross
14 Jesus is placed in the tomb

Lord, by your cross and resurrection
you have set us free.
You are the Saviour of the world.

Teach me to be generous,
Teach me to love and serve
    you as you deserve,
To give and not to count the cost.
To fight and not to heed the wounds.
To toil and not to seek for rest.
To labour and to look for no reward.
Save that of knowing that
    I do your holy will.
Amen

Ignatius Loyola

For a good life

Give us, Lord,
a humble, quiet, peaceable,
patient, tender, charitable mind
and in all our thoughts, words and deeds
a taste of your Holy Spirit.

Give us, Lord,
a lively faith,
a firm hope,
a warm charity,
a love of you.
Take from us all lukewarmness in prayer.
Give us warmth and delight
in thinking of you
and your grace and tender compassion to us.
The things that we pray for, Lord,
give us grace to work for,
through Jesus Christ, our Lord.

Thomas More

Prayers for the Dead

Eternal rest grant unto them, O Lord,
and let perpetual light shine upon them.

May their souls and the souls of all the faithful
departed, through the mercy of God
rest in peace.
Amen.

Remember those who have died in the peace of
Christ and all the dead whose faith is known to you
alone.
Father, in your mercy grant also to us, your
children,
to enter into our heavenly inheritance
in the company of the Virgin Mary,
the Mother of God, and your apostles and saints.
Then, in your kingdom,
freed from the corruption of sin and death
we shall sing your glory with every creature
through Christ our Lord,
through whom you give us everything that is good.

86

For Someone I know who has Died

_____

_____

_____

_____

_____

_____

_____

_____

In Time of Sickness

O Lord,
Look kindly on those who are sick.
Give new strength to their minds and bodies.
Ease out their sufferings.
Free them from sin and temptation.
Sustain all the sick with your power.
Assist all who care for the sick.
Give life and health to those
on whom we lay our hands in your name.

Lord Jesus Christ, our Redeemer,
by the power of the Holy Spirit
ease the suffering of those who are ill or in pain,
and make them well again in mind and body.
In your loving kindness forgive their sins
and grant them full health,
so that they may be restored to your service.
You are Lord for ever and ever.
Amen.

A Prayer of Thanks for Life and Health

O God, thank you for making me as I am.
Thank you for health and strength;
For eyes to see;
For ears to hear;
For hands to work;
For feet to walk and run;
For a mind to think;
For a memory to remember;
For a heart to love.
Thank you for parents who are kind to me;
Friends who are true to me;
Teachers who are patient with me.
Thank you for this wonderful life.
Help me to try to deserve all your gifts
a little more.
This I ask for Jesus' sake.
Amen.

The Divine Praises

Blessed be God.

Blessed be his holy Name.

Blessed be Jesus Christ, true God and true man.

Blessed be the name of Jesus.

Blessed be his most Sacred Heart.

Blessed be his most Precious Blood.

Blessed be Jesus in the most Blessed Sacrament
of the Altar.

Blessed be the Holy Spirit, the Paraclete.

Blessed be the great Mother of God, Mary most
holy.

Blessed be her holy and immaculate Conception.

Blessed be her glorious Assumption.

Blessed be the name of Mary, Virgin and Mother.

Blessed be Saint Joseph, her most chaste spouse.

Blessed be God, in his angels and in his saints.

O Lord, Support Us

O Lord, support us all the day long,
until the shadows lengthen,
and the evening comes,
and the busy world is hushed,
and the fever of life is over,
and our work is done.
Then, Lord, in your mercy,
grant us safe lodging,
a holy rest,
and peace at the last;
through Jesus Christ our Lord.
Amen.

Henry Newman

A Time for Everything

Everything that happens in this world
happens at the time God chooses.

He sets the time for birth and the time for death,
the time for planting and the time for pulling up,
the time for killing and the time for healing,
the time for tearing down and the time for
building.

He sets the time for sorrow and the time for joy,
the time for mourning and the time for dancing,
the time for making love and the time for not
making love,
the time for kissing and the time for not kissing.

He sets the time for finding and the time for losing,
the time for saving and the time for throwing away,
the time for tearing and the time for mending,
the time for silence and the time for talk.

He sets the time for love and the time for hate,
the time for war and the time for peace.
What do we gain from all our work?
(Ecclesiastes 3:1-9)

———

Reflections on my Confirmation Day

_____

_____

_____

_____

_____

_____

_____

_____